Christian Book Series Self Help Bible Study Guide on Hell

KJV Bible Based Verses & Lessons for Men, Women, Couples, Teens, Kids, & Beginners

by Brian Mahoney

TABLE OF CONTENTS

Part 1 INTRODUCTION 10

Part 2 OT Bible Verses on Hell 19

Part 3 OT Bible Verses on Hell 24

Part 4 NT Bible Verses on Hell 30

Part 5 NT Bible Verses on Hell 41

Part 6 NT Bible Verses on Hell 48

Part 7 Bible Life Lesson on Hell 60

Part 8 Top 10 Bible Verses on Hell 67

Part 9 Bible Quiz on Hell 74

Part 10 CONCLUSION 86

About the Author

Brian Mahoney has spent a quarter century preaching and teaching the word of God in non denominational Churches of Christ through out the United States.

He served two overseas tours in the United States Army, then worked for the Government for almost two decades and has a IT degree in Computer Programming and is completing another degree in Business.

He has 2 sons. Both his sons accepted the gospel of Jesus Christ and were baptized as teenagers. Attending the University of Virginia, Columbia Law School and Radford University. Between them they have gone on to get degrees in Law, Physical Therapy and Engineering.

Disclaimer Notice

This book was written as a guide and for information, educational and entertainment purposes only. No warranties of any kind are expressed or implied.

Readers acknowledge that the author is not engaging in the rendering of legal, financial, medical or professional advice, and the information in this book is not meant to take the place of any professional advice. If advice is needed in any of these fields, you are advised to seek the services of a professional.

While the author has attempted to make the information in this book as accurate as possible, no guarantee is given as to the accuracy or currency of any individual item. Laws and procedures related to business, health and well being are constantly changing.

Therefore, in no event shall the author of this book be liable for any special, indirect, or consequential damages or any damages whatsoever in connection with the use of the information herein provided.

All Rights Reserved

No part of this book may be used or reproduced in any manner whatsoever without the written permission of the author.

Copyright © 2022 Brian Mahoney
All rights reserved.

DEDICATION

This book is dedicated to my Father

Ulester Love Mahoney Sr.

He instilled a love for God, and taught

as much by his actions as he did with his words.

ACKNOWLEDGMENTS

I WOULD LIKE TO ACKNOWLEDGE ALL THE HARD WORK OF THE MEN AND WOMEN OF THE UNITED STATES MILITARY, WHO RISK THEIR LIVES ON A DAILY BASIS, TO MAKE THE WORLD A SAFER PLACE.

PART 1
INTRODUCTION

PART 1 INTRODUCTION

I want to thank you for purchasing

Christian Book Series Self Help Bible Study Guide on Hell, KJV Bible Based Verses & Lessons for Men, Women, Couples, Teens, Kids, & Beginners

This is just one of a series of books I have created to give bible answers to bible topics or questions.

With this book you will Discover...

* The best Old Testament Bible Verses on on this amazing topic!
* The best New Testament Bible Verses on this amazing topic!
* We reveal the top 10 Scriptures on **Hell** voted online from Christians around the world!
* A Bible chapter, set of scriptures or story to best illustrate & understand **Hell**!
* A quick & easy quiz to aid in retention of all the knowledge you discover.

PART 1 INTRODUCTION

Just a few of the many uses...

* A perfect gift for family and friends
* Deepen your personal Bible Study
* A teaching aid for Bible Study Classes
* A teaching aid for counseling
* Use for morning meditation
* Use the AUDIO BOOK version for sleep affirmation

This book will help beginners to get off of milk and begin to eat meat!

Hebrews 5:12

"For when for the time ye ought to be teachers, ye have need that one teach you again which be the first principles of the oracles of God; and are become such as have need of milk, and not of strong meat."

1 Peter 3:15

" But sanctify the Lord God in your hearts: and be ready always to give an answer to every man that asketh you a reason of the hope that is in you with meekness and fear:"

PART 1 INTRODUCTION

Now is the time to grow spiritually! Discover more of what the Bible says about **this important topic,** so you can be ready to share the Good News when the opportunity arises!

Throughout this book at the end of several sections will be a Bible Bonus Section!

and the first of these will be a bonus Lesson on bible basics: The Bible, The Church & Christians!

The bible is a book of books, consisting of the Old and New Testaments.

The Bible takes its name from the Latin Biblia ('book' or 'books') which comes from the Greek Ta Biblia ('the books') traced to the Phoenician port city of Gebal, known as Byblos to the Greeks. Writing became associated with Byblos as an exporter of papyrus (used in writing) and the Greek name for papyrus was bublos.

Now if you ever get the chance to visit Epcot Center at Walt Disney World Florida, the Phoenician section of the Space Earth ride will take on a whole new meaning!

PART 1 INTRODUCTION

The bible is divided into sections and they are:

The Old Testament
It's Sections:
The Law: Genesis - Deuteronomy
History: Joshua - Esther
Poetry: Job - Song of Solomon
Major prophets: Isaiah - Daniel
Minor prophets: Hosea - Malachi

The New Testament
It's Sections:
The Gospels: Matthew - John
History: Acts
The Epistles: Romans - Jude
Prophecy: Revelation

What is the Church?

(eck la see a) the church the called out
Ekklesia is a Greek word defined as "a called-out assembly or congregation." Ekklesia is commonly translated as "church" in the New Testament. For example, Acts 11:26 says that "Barnabas and Saul met with the church [ekklesia]" in Antioch.

PART 1 INTRODUCTION

Why are we called Christians?

Acts 11:26

And when he had found him, he brought him unto Antioch. And it came to pass, that a whole year they assembled themselves with the church, and taught much people. And the disciples were called **Christians** first in Antioch.

Why do we assemble for worship service?

Hebrews 10:25-26

25 Not forsaking the assembling of ourselves together, as the manner of some is; but exhorting one another: and so much the more, as ye see the day approaching.

26 For if we sin wilfully after that we have received the knowledge of the truth, there remaineth no more sacrifice for sins,

PART 1 INTRODUCTION

Why do we worship on Sunday?

1 Corinthians 16:2

2 Upon the first day of the week let every one of you lay by him in store, as God hath prospered him, that there be no gatherings when I come.

Acts 20:6-7

6 And we sailed away from Philippi after the days of unleavened bread, and came unto them to Troas in five days; where we abode seven days.

7 And upon the first day of the week, when the disciples came together to break bread, Paul preached unto them, ready to depart on the morrow; and continued his speech until midnight.

So they were there seven days, and they did something on the first day they did not do on the others, and that is they came together to break bread and Paul preached to them.

PART 1 INTRODUCTION

Why should we continue to read and study the Bible? Because....

"16 All scripture is given by inspiration of God, and is profitable for doctrine, for reproof, for correction, for instruction in righteousness:

17 That the man of God may be perfect, thoroughly furnished unto all good works."

2 Timothy 3:16-17

This concludes the Introduction... Now let's get started with Bible Verses about **Hell**.

ENCOURAGING SCRIPTURES OLD TESTAMENT BIBLE BONUS

ENCOURAGING SCRIPTURES
OLD TESTAMENT

At some point we all need encouragement. There is nothing like the wisdom of Word of God to give us encouragement.

"Encouraging Scriptures" was written not only to give you encouragement, but to help you to learn the Bible. That is why I found a scripture from every book in the Old Testament and every book in the New Testament.

While most of the scriptures deal with encouragement, some of the scriptures help to summarize the point or meaning of a particular book.

We are told to be ready to give an answer. The Encouraging Scriptures chapters help you to be better prepared for a wide range of questions one might have for the hope of your salvation.

God bless and protect you.

Brian Mahoney

ENCOURAGING SCRIPTURES
OLD TESTAMENT

Genensis

Genesis 50:20 (KJV)

But as for you, ye thought evil against me; but God meant it unto good, to bring to pass, as it is this day, to save much people alive.

Exodus

Exodus 20:3 (KJV)

Thou shalt have no other gods before me.

Leviticus

Leviticus 18:22 (KJV)

Thou shalt not lie with mankind, as with womankind: it is abomination.

Numbers

Numbers 23:19 (KJV)

God is not a man, that he should lie; neither the son of man, that he should repent: hath he said, and shall he not do it? or hath he spoken, and shall he not make it good?

ENCOURAGING SCRIPTURES
OLD TESTAMENT

Deuteronomy

Deuteronomy 28:13 (KJV)

And the Lord shall make thee the head, and not the tail; and thou shalt be above only, and thou shalt not be beneath; if that thou hearken unto the commandments of the Lord thy God, which I command thee this day, to observe and to do them:

Joshua

Joshua 1:7 (KJV)

Only be thou strong and very courageous, that thou mayest observe to do according to all the law, which Moses my servant commanded thee: turn not from it to the right hand or to the left, that thou mayest prosper withersoever thou goest.

Judges

Judges 4:9 (KJV)

And she said, I will surely go with thee: notwithstanding the journey that thou takest shall not be for thine honour; for the Lord shall sell Sisera into the hand of a woman. And Deborah arose, and went with Barak to Kedesh.

ENCOURAGING SCRIPTURES
OLD TESTAMENT

1 Samuel

1 Samuel 15:23 (KJV)

For rebellion is as the sin of witchcraft, and stubbornness is as iniquity and idolatry. Because thou hast rejected the word of the Lord, he hath also rejected thee from being king.

2 Samuel

2 Samuel 12:13 (KJV)

13 And David said unto Nathan, I have sinned against the Lord. And Nathan said unto David, The Lord also hath put away thy sin; thou shalt not die.

1 Kings

1 Kings 8:23 (KJV)

And he said, Lord God of Israel, there is no God like thee

, in heaven above, or on earth beneath, who keepest covenant and mercy with thy servants that walk before thee with all their heart:

ENCOURAGING SCRIPTURES
OLD TESTAMENT

2 Kings

2 Kings 5:11-14 (KJV)

But Naaman was wroth, and went away, and said, Behold, I thought, He will surely come out to me, and stand, and call on the name of the Lord his God, and strike his hand over the place, and recover the leper. Are not Abana and Pharpar, rivers of Damascus, better than all the waters of Israel? may I not wash in them, and be clean? So he turned and went away in a rage. And his servants came near, and spake unto him, and said, My father, if the prophet had bid thee do some great thing, wouldest thou not have done it? how much rather then, when he saith to thee, Wash, and be clean? Then went he down, and dipped himself seven times in Jordan, according to the saying of the man of God: and his flesh came again like unto the flesh of a little child, and he was clean.

1 Chronicles

1 Chronicles 4:10 (KJV)

And Jabez called on the God of Israel, saying, Oh that thou wouldest bless me indeed, and enlarge my coast, and that thine hand might be with me, and that thou wouldest keep me from evil, that it may not grieve me! And God granted him that which he requested.

ENCOURAGING SCRIPTURES
OLD TESTAMENT

2 Chronicles

2 Chronicles 7:14 (KJV)

If my people, which are called by my name, shall humble themselves, and pray, and seek my face, and turn from their wicked ways; then will I hear from heaven, and will forgive their sin, and will heal their land.

Ezra

Ezra 3:11 (KJV)

And they sang together by course in praising and giving thanks unto the Lord; because he is good, for his mercy endureth for ever toward Israel. And all the people shouted with a great shout, when they praised the Lord, because the foundation of the house of the Lord was laid.

Nehemiah

Nehemiah 4:4 (KJV)

Hear, O our God; for we are despised: and turn their reproach upon their own head, and give them for a prey in the land of captivity:

ENCOURAGING SCRIPTURES
OLD TESTAMENT

Esther

Esther 4:14 (KJV)

For if thou altogether holdest thy peace at this time, then shall there enlargement and deliverance arise to the Jews from another place; but thou and thy father's house shall be destroyed: and who knoweth whether thou art come to the kingdom for such a time as this?

Job

Job 42:1-2 (KJV)

Then Job answered the Lord, and said, I know that thou canst do every thing, and that no thought can be withholden from thee.

PART 2
OLD TESTAMENT BIBLE VERSES

PART 2 OLD TESTAMENT BIBLE VERSES

Law

Numbers 16:33 KJV / 247

33 They, and all that appertained to them, went down alive into the pit, and the earth closed upon them: and they perished from among the congregation.

Prophets

Daniel 12:2 KJV / 465

2 And many of them that sleep in the dust of the earth shall awake, some to everlasting life, and some to shame and everlasting contempt.

Jeremiah 7:31 KJV / 274

31 And they have built the high places of Tophet, which is in the valley of the son of Hinnom, to burn their sons and their daughters in the fire; which I commanded them not, neither came it into my heart.

PART 2 OLD TESTAMENT BIBLE VERSES

Ezekiel 18:4 KJV / 236

4 Behold, all souls are mine; as the soul of the father, so also the soul of the son is mine: the soul that sinneth, it shall die.

Ezekiel 18:20 KJV / 313

20 The soul that sinneth, it shall die. The son shall not bear the iniquity of the father, neither shall the father bear the iniquity of the son: the righteousness of the righteous shall be upon him, and the wickedness of the wicked shall be upon him.

Ezekiel 31:17 KJV / 263

17 They also went down into hell with him unto them that be slain with the sword; and they that were his arm, that dwelt under his shadow in the midst of the heathen.

Isaiah 66:24 KJV / 295

24 And they shall go forth, and look upon the carcases of the men that have transgressed against me: for their worm shall not die, neither shall their fire be quenched; and they shall be an abhorring unto all flesh.

PART 2 OLD TESTAMENT BIBLE VERSES

Isaiah 14:9 KJV / 285

9 Hell from beneath is moved for thee to meet thee at thy coming: it stirreth up the dead for thee, even all the chief ones of the earth; it hath raised up from their thrones all the kings of the nations.

Isaiah 5:14 KJV / 265

14 Therefore hell hath enlarged herself, and opened her mouth without measure: and their glory, and their multitude, and their pomp, and he that rejoiceth, shall descend into it.

Isaiah 47:14 KJV / 199

14 Behold, they shall be as stubble; the fire shall burn them; they shall not deliver themselves from the power of the flame: there shall not be a coal to warm at, nor fire to sit before it.

Encouraging Scriptures Old Testament BIBLE BONUS 2

Encouraging Scriptures
Old Testament

Psalm

Psalm 111:9

He sent redemption unto his people: he hath commanded his covenant for ever: holy and reverend is His name.

Proverbs

Proverbs 18:21 (KJV)

Death and life are in the power of the tongue: and they that love it shall eat the fruit thereof.

Ecclesiastes

Ecclesiastes 8:11 (KJV)

Because sentence against an evil work is not executed speedily, therefore the heart of the sons of men is fully set in them to do evil.

Song of Solomon

Song of Solomon 8:7 Contemporary English Version (CEV)

Love cannot be drowned by oceans or floods; it cannot be bought, no matter what is offered.

Encouraging Scriptures
Old Testament

Isaiah

Isaiah 55:9 (KJV)

For as the heavens are higher than the earth, so are my ways higher than your ways, and my thoughts than your thoughts.

Jeremiah

Jeremiah 29:11 (KJV)

For I know the thoughts that I think toward you, saith the Lord, thoughts of peace, and not of evil, to give you an expected end.

Lamentations

Lamentations 3:22-23 (KJV)

It is of the Lord's mercies that we are not consumed, because his compassions fail not. They are new every morning: great is thy faithfulness.

Encouraging Scriptures
Old Testament

Ezekiel

Ezekiel 25:17 (KJV)

And I will execute great vengeance upon them with furious rebukes; and they shall know that I am the Lord, when I shall lay my vengeance upon them.

Daniel

Daniel 10:12

Then said he unto me, Fear not, Daniel: for from the first day that thou didst set thine heart to understand, and to chasten thyself before thy God, thy words were heard, and I am come for thy words.

Hosea

Hosea 4:6 (KJV)

My people are destroyed for lack of knowledge: because thou hast rejected knowledge, I will also reject thee, that thou shalt be no priest to me: seeing thou hast forgotten the law of thy God, I will also forget thy children.

Encouraging Scriptures
Old Testament

Joel

Joel 2:25 (KJV)

And I will restore to you the years that the locust hath eaten, the cankerworm, and the caterpiller, and the palmerworm, my great army which I sent among you.

Amos

Amos 3:3 (KJV)

Can two walk together, except they be agreed?

Obadiah

Obadiah 4 (KJV)

Though thou exalt thyself as the eagle, and though thou set thy nest among the stars, thence will I bring thee down, saith the Lord.

Jonah

Jonah 2:9-10 (KJV)

But I will sacrifice unto thee with the voice of thanksgiving; I will pay that that I have vowed. Salvation is of the Lord. And the Lord spake unto the fish, and it vomited out Jonah upon the dry land.

Encouraging Scriptures
Old Testament

Micah

Micah 6:8 (KJV)

He hath shewed thee, O man, what is good; and what doth the Lord require of thee, but to do justly, and to love mercy, and to walk humbly with thy God?

Nahum

Nahum 1:3 (KJV)

The Lord is slow to anger, and great in power, and will not at all acquit the wicked: the Lord hath his way in the whirlwind and in the storm, and the clouds are the dust of his feet.

Habakkuk

Habakkuk 2:2 (KJV)

And the Lord answered me, and said, Write the vision, and make it plain upon tables, that he may run that readeth it.

Encouraging Scriptures
Old Testament

Zephaniah

Zephaniah 3:17 (KJV)

The Lord thy God in the midst of thee is mighty; he will save, he will rejoice over thee with joy; he will rest in his love, he will joy over thee with singing.

Haggai

Haggai 2:9 (KJV)

The glory of this latter house shall be greater than of the former, saith the Lord of hosts: and in this place will I give peace, saith the Lord of hosts.

Zechariah

Zechariah 4:6 (KJV)

Then he answered and spake unto me, saying, This is the word of the Lord unto Zerubbabel, saying, Not by might, nor by power, but by my spirit, saith the Lord of hosts.

Encouraging Scriptures
Old Testament

Malachi

Malachi 3:10 (KJV)

Bring ye all the tithes into the storehouse, that there may be meat in mine house, and prove me now herewith, saith the Lord of hosts, if I will not open you the windows of heaven, and pour you out a blessing, that there shall not be room enough to receive it.

PART 3
OLD TESTAMENT
BIBLE VERSES

PART 3 OLD TESTAMENT BIBLE VERSES

Poetry

Ecclesiastes 9:5 KJV / 274

5 For the living know that they shall die: but the dead know not any thing, neither have they any more a reward; for the memory of them is forgotten.

Ecclesiastes 9:10 KJV / 244

10 Whatsoever thy hand findeth to do, do it with thy might; for there is no work, nor device, nor knowledge, nor wisdom, in the grave, whither thou goest.

The book of Proverbs

Proverbs 15:24 KJV / 421

24 The way of life is above to the wise, that he may depart from hell beneath.

Proverbs 23:14 KJV / 390

14 Thou shalt beat him with the rod, and shalt deliver his soul from hell.

PART 3 OLD TESTAMENT BIBLE VERSES

Proverbs 15:11 KJV / 344

11 Hell and destruction are before the Lord: how much more then the hearts of the children of men?

Proverbs 27:20 KJV / 236

20 Hell and destruction are never full; so the eyes of man are never satisfied.

Proverbs 9:18 KJV / 294

18 But he knoweth not that the dead are there; and that her guests are in the depths of hell.

The book of Psalms

Psalm 16:10 KJV / 461

10 For thou wilt not leave my soul in hell; neither wilt thou suffer thine Holy One to see corruption.

PART 3 OLD TESTAMENT BIBLE VERSES

Psalm 9:17 KJV / 456

17 The wicked shall be turned into hell, and all the nations that forget God.

Psalm 145:20 KJV / 343

20 The Lord preserveth all them that love him: but all the wicked will he destroy.

Psalm 139:8 KJV / 337

8 If I ascend up into heaven, thou art there: if I make my bed in hell, behold, thou art there.

Psalm 86:13 KJV / 334

13 For great is thy mercy toward me: and thou hast delivered my soul from the lowest hell.

Psalm 37:20 KJV / 206

20 But the wicked shall perish, and the enemies of the Lord shall be as the fat of lambs: they shall consume; into smoke shall they consume away.

PART 3 OLD TESTAMENT BIBLE VERSES

Psalm 146:4 KJV / 204

4 His breath goeth forth, he returneth to his earth; in that very day his thoughts perish.

Encouraging Scriptures

New Testament
BIBLE BONUS 3

Encouraging Scriptures
New Testament

Matthew

Matthew 7:21 (KJV)

Not every one that saith unto me, Lord, Lord, shall enter into the kingdom of heaven; but he that doeth the will of my Father which is in heaven.

Mark

Mark 7:7 (KJV)

Howbeit in vain do they worship me, teaching for doctrines the commandments of men.

Luke

Luke 6:46 (KJV)

And why call ye me, Lord, Lord, and do not the things which I say?

John

John 4:24 (KJV)

God is a Spirit: and they that worship him must worship him in spirit and in truth.

Encouraging Scriptures
New Testament

Acts

Acts 14:15 (KJV)

And saying, Sirs, why do ye these things? We also are men of like passions with you, and preach unto you that ye should turn from these vanities unto the living God, which made heaven, and earth, and the sea, and all things that are therein:

Romans

Romans 8:28 (KJV)

And we know that all things work together for good to them that love God, to them who are the called according to his purpose.

1 Corinthians

1 Corinthians 11:25 (KJV)

25 After the same manner also he took the cup, when he had supped, saying, this cup is the new testament in my blood: this do ye, as oft as ye drink it, in remembrance of me.

Encouraging Scriptures
New Testament

2 Corinthians

2 Corinthians 9:7

Every man according as he purposeth in his heart, so let him give; not grudgingly, or of necessity: for God loveth a cheerful giver.

Galatians

Galatians 6:7-8 (KJV)

Be not deceived; God is not mocked: for whatsoever a man soweth, that shall he also reap. For he that soweth to his flesh shall of the flesh reap corruption; but he that soweth to the Spirit shall of the Spirit reap life everlasting.

Ephesians

Ephesians 4:4-6

There is one body, and one Spirit, even as ye are called in one hope of your calling;One Lord, one faith, one baptism,One God and Father of all, who is above all, and through all, and in you all.

Encouraging Scriptures
New Testament

Philippians

Philippians 4:13 (KJV)

I can do all things through Christ which strengtheneth me.

Colossians

Colossians 3:23 (KJV)

And whatsoever ye do, do it heartily, as to the Lord, and not unto men;

1 Thessalonians

1 Thessalonians 4:16 (KJV)

For the Lord himself shall descend from heaven with a shout, with the voice of the archangel, and with the trump of God: and the dead in Christ shall rise first:

2 Thessalonians

2 Thessalonians 3:10 (KJV)

For even when we were with you, this we commanded you, that if any would not work, neither should he eat.

Encouraging Scriptures
New Testament

1 Timothy

1 Timothy 5:8 (KJV)

But if any provide not for his own, and specially for those of his own house, he hath denied the faith, and is worse than an infidel.

2 Timothy

2 Timothy 3:16-17 (KJV)

All scripture is given by inspiration of God, and is profitable for doctrine, for reproof, for correction, for instruction in righteousness: That the man of God may be perfect, thoroughly furnished unto all good works.

Titus

Titus 1:6-9 (KJV)

If any be blameless, the husband of one wife, having faithful children not accused of riot or unruly. For a bishop must be blameless, as the steward of God; not selfwilled, not soon angry, not given to wine, no striker, not given to filthy lucre; But a lover of hospitality, a lover of good men, sober, just, holy, temperate; Holding fast the faithful word as he hath been taught, that he may be able by sound doctrine both to exhort and to convince the gainsayers.

PART 4
NEW TESTAMENT
BIBLE VERSES

PART 4 NEW TESTAMENT BIBLE VERSES

The Gospels
The book of Matthew

Matthew 10:28 KJV / 1,534

28 And fear not them which kill the body, but are not able to kill the soul: but rather fear him which is able to destroy both soul and body in hell.

Matthew 25:46 KJV / 1,444
46 And these shall go away into everlasting punishment: but the righteous into life eternal.

Matthew 25:41 KJV / 1,139
41 Then shall he say also unto them on the left hand, Depart from me, ye cursed, into everlasting fire, prepared for the devil and his angels:

Matthew 5:22 KJV / 1,061

22 But I say unto you, That whosoever is angry with his brother without a cause shall be in danger of the judgment: and whosoever shall say to his brother, Raca, shall be in danger of the council: but whosoever shall say, Thou fool, shall be in danger of hell fire.

PART 4 NEW TESTAMENT BIBLE VERSES

Matthew 3:12 KJV / 422

12 Whose fan is in his hand, and he will throughly purge his floor, and gather his wheat into the garner; but he will burn up the chaff with unquenchable fire.

Matthew 8:12 KJV / 434

12 But the children of the kingdom shall be cast out into outer darkness: there shall be weeping and gnashing of teeth.

Matthew 11:23 KJV / 313

23 And thou, Capernaum, which art exalted unto heaven, shalt be brought down to hell: for if the mighty works, which have been done in thee, had been done in Sodom, it would have remained until this day.

Matthew 13:50 KJV / 908

50 And shall cast them into the furnace of fire: there shall be wailing and gnashing of teeth.

PART 4 NEW TESTAMENT BIBLE VERSES

Matthew 16:18 KJV / 539

18 And I say also unto thee, That thou art Peter, and upon this rock I will build my church; and the gates of hell shall not prevail against it.

Matthew 23:15 KJV / 264

15 Woe unto you, scribes and Pharisees, hypocrites! for ye compass sea and land to make one proselyte, and when he is made, ye make him twofold more the child of hell than yourselves.

Matthew 23:33 KJV / 702

33 Ye serpents, ye generation of vipers, how can ye escape the damnation of hell?

Matthew 24:51 KJV / 257

51 And shall cut him asunder, and appoint him his portion with the hypocrites: there shall be weeping and gnashing of teeth.

PART 4 NEW TESTAMENT BIBLE VERSES

Matthew 5:29-30 KJV / 252

29 And if thy right eye offend thee, pluck it out, and cast it from thee: for it is profitable for thee that one of thy members should perish, and not that thy whole body should be cast into hell.
30 And if thy right hand offend thee, cut it off, and cast it from thee: for it is profitable for thee that one of thy members should perish, and not that thy whole body should be cast into hell.

Matthew 7:13-14 KJV / 391

13 Enter ye in at the strait gate: for wide is the gate, and broad is the way, that leadeth to destruction, and many there be which go in thereat:

14 Because strait is the gate, and narrow is the way, which leadeth unto life, and few there be that find it.

Matthew 7:21-23 KJV / 386

21 Not every one that saith unto me, Lord, Lord, shall enter into the kingdom of heaven; but he that doeth the will of my Father which is in heaven.

PART 4 NEW TESTAMENT BIBLE VERSES

22 Many will say to me in that day, Lord, Lord, have we not prophesied in thy name? and in thy name have cast out devils? and in thy name done many wonderful works?

23 And then will I profess unto them, I never knew you: depart from me, ye that work iniquity.

Matthew 13:41-42 KJV / 349

41 The Son of man shall send forth his angels, and they shall gather out of his kingdom all things that offend, and them which do iniquity;

42 And shall cast them into a furnace of fire: **there shall be wailing and gnashing of teeth.**

Matthew 18:8-9 KJV / 308

8 Wherefore if thy hand or thy foot offend thee, cut them off, and cast them from thee: it is better for thee to enter into life halt or maimed, rather than having two hands or two feet to be cast into everlasting fire.
9 And if thine eye offend thee, pluck it out, and cast it from thee: it is better for thee to enter into life with one eye, rather than having two eyes to be cast into hell fire.

PART 4 NEW TESTAMENT BIBLE VERSES

The book of Mark

Mark 9:43-48 KJV / 596

43 And if thy hand offend thee, cut it off: it is better for thee to enter into life maimed, than having two hands to go into hell, into the fire that never shall be quenched:

44 Where their worm dieth not, and the fire is not quenched.

45 And if thy foot offend thee, cut it off: it is better for thee to enter halt into life, than having two feet to be cast into hell, into the fire that never shall be quenched:

46 Where their worm dieth not, and the fire is not quenched.

47 And if thine eye offend thee, pluck it out: it is better for thee to enter into the kingdom of God with one eye, than having two eyes to be cast into hell fire:

48 Where their worm dieth not, and the fire is not quenched.

PART 4 NEW TESTAMENT BIBLE VERSES

The Book of Luke

Luke 3:17 KJV / 245

17 Whose fan is in his hand, and he will throughly purge his floor, and will gather the wheat into his garner; but the chaff he will burn with fire unquenchable.

Luke 10:15 KJV / 397

15 And thou, Capernaum, which art exalted to heaven, shalt be thrust down to hell.

Luke 12:5 KJV / 537

5 But I will forewarn you whom ye shall fear: Fear him, which after he hath killed hath power to cast into hell; yea, I say unto you, Fear him.

Luke 16:23-24 KJV / 607

23 And in hell he lift up his eyes, being in torments, and seeth Abraham afar off, and Lazarus in his bosom.

PART 4 NEW TESTAMENT BIBLE VERSES

24 And he cried and said, Father Abraham, have mercy on me, and send Lazarus, that he may dip the tip of his finger in water, and cool my tongue; for I am tormented in this flame.

Luke 23:43 KJV / 354

43 And Jesus said unto him, Verily I say unto thee, Today shalt thou be with me in paradise.

The book of John

John 3:13 KJV / 233

13 And no man hath ascended up to heaven, but he that came down from heaven, even the Son of man which is in heaven.

John 3:36 KJV / 517

36 He that believeth on the Son hath everlasting life: and he that believeth not the Son shall not see life; but the wrath of God abideth on him.

PART 4 NEW TESTAMENT BIBLE VERSES

John 3:16-18 KJV / 622

16 For God so loved the world, that he gave his only begotten Son, that whosoever believeth in him should not perish, but have everlasting life.

17 For God sent not his Son into the world to condemn the world; but that the world through him might be saved.

18 He that believeth on him is not condemned: but he that believeth not is condemned already, because he hath not believed in the name of the only begotten Son of God.

John 5:28-29 KJV / 300

28 Marvel not at this: for the hour is coming, in the which all that are in the graves shall hear his voice,

29 And shall come forth; they that have done good, unto the resurrection of life; and they that have done evil, unto the resurrection of damnation.

Encouraging Scriptures New Testament BIBLE BONUS 4

Encouraging Scriptures
New Testament

Philemon

Philemon 15-16 (KJV)

For perhaps he therefore departed for a season, that thou shouldest receive him for ever; Not now as a servant, but above a servant, a brother beloved, specially to me, but how much more unto thee, both in the flesh, and in the Lord?

Hebrews

Hebrews 12:11 Living Bible (TLB)

Being punished isn't enjoyable while it is happening—it hurts! But afterwards we can see the result, a quiet growth in grace and character.

James

James 4:2-3 (KJV)

Ye lust, and have not: ye kill, and desire to have, and cannot obtain: ye fight and war, yet ye have not, because ye ask not. Ye ask, and receive not, because ye ask amiss, that ye may consume it upon your lusts.

Encouraging Scriptures
New Testament

1 Peter

1 Peter 3:15 (KJV)

But sanctify the Lord God in your hearts: and be ready always to give an answer to every man that asketh you a reason of the hope that is in you with meekness and fear:.

2 Peter

2 Peter 3:9 (KJV)

The Lord is not slack concerning his promise, as some men count slackness; but is longsuffering to us-ward, not willing that any should perish, but that all should come to repentance.

1 John

1 John 1:10 (KJV)

If we say that we have not sinned, we make him a liar, and his word is not in us.

Encouraging Scriptures
New Testament

2 John

2 John 6 (KJV)

And this is love, that we walk after his commandments. This is the commandment, That, as ye have heard from the beginning, ye should walk in it.

3 John

3 John 2 (KJV)

Beloved, I wish above all things that thou mayest prosper and be in health, even as thy soul prospereth.

Jude

Jude 24-25 (KJV)

Now unto him that is able to keep you from falling, and to present you faultless before the presence of his glory with exceeding joy, To the only wise God our Saviour, be glory and majesty, dominion and power, both now and ever. Amen.

Encouraging Scriptures
New Testament

Revelation

Revelation 2:10 (KJV)

Fear none of those things which thou shalt suffer: behold, the devil shall cast some of you into prison, that ye may be tried; and ye shall have tribulation ten days: be thou faithful unto death, and I will give thee a crown of life.

Revelation 3:15-16 (KJV)

I know thy works, that thou art neither cold nor hot: I would thou wert cold or hot. So then because thou art lukewarm, and neither cold nor hot, I will spue thee out of my mouth.

Revelation 21:8 English Standard Version (ESV)

But as for the cowardly, the faithless, the detestable, as for murderers, the sexually immoral, sorcerers, idolaters, and all liars, their portion will be in the lake that burns with fire and sulfur, which is the second death."

PART 5
NEW TESTAMENT
BIBLE VERSES

PART 5 NEW TESTAMENT BIBLE VERSES

History

The book of Acts

Acts 2:27 KJV / 489

27 Because thou wilt not leave my soul in hell, neither wilt thou suffer thine Holy One to see corruption.

Acts 2:31 KJV / 396

31 He seeing this before spake of the resurrection of Christ, that his soul was not left in hell, neither his flesh did see corruption.

Acts 24:15 KJV / 242

15 And have hope toward God, which they themselves also allow, that there shall be a resurrection of the dead, both of the just and unjust.

Acts 4:12 KJV / 241

12 Neither is there salvation in any other: for there is none other name under heaven given among men, whereby we must be saved.

PART 5 NEW TESTAMENT BIBLE VERSES

The Epistles

James 3:6 KJV / 337

6 And the tongue is a fire, a world of iniquity: so is the tongue among our members, that it defileth the whole body, and setteth on fire the course of nature; and it is set on fire of hell.

Romans 6:23 KJV / 1,212

23 For the wages of sin is death; but the gift of God is eternal life through Jesus Christ our Lord.

1 John 4:8 KJV / 189

8 He that loveth not knoweth not God; for God is love.

Hebrews 9:27 KJV / 529

27 And as it is appointed unto men once to die, but after this the judgment:

PART 5 NEW TESTAMENT BIBLE VERSES

Hebrews 10:26-31 KJV / 331

26 For if we sin wilfully after that we have received the knowledge of the truth, there remaineth no more sacrifice for sins,

27 But a certain fearful looking for of judgment and fiery indignation, which shall devour the adversaries.

28 He that despised Moses' law died without mercy under two or three witnesses:

29 Of how much sorer punishment, suppose ye, shall he be thought worthy, who hath trodden under foot the Son of God, and hath counted the blood of the covenant, wherewith he was sanctified, an unholy thing, and hath done despite unto the Spirit of grace?

30 For we know him that hath said, Vengeance belongeth unto me, I will recompense, saith the Lord. And again, The Lord shall judge his people.

31 It is a fearful thing to fall into the hands of the living God.

PART 5 NEW TESTAMENT BIBLE VERSES

2 Peter 2:4 KJV / 844

4 For if God spared not the angels that sinned, but cast them down to hell, and delivered them into chains of darkness, to be reserved unto judgment;

2 Peter 2:17 KJV / 195

17 These are wells without water, clouds that are carried with a tempest; to whom the mist of darkness is reserved for ever.

2 Peter 3:9 KJV / 386

9 The Lord is not slack concerning his promise, as some men count slackness; but is longsuffering to us-ward, not willing that any should perish, but that all should come to repentance.

2 Thessalonians 1:8-9 KJV / 244

8 In flaming fire taking vengeance on them that know not God, and that obey not the gospel of our Lord Jesus Christ:

PART 5 NEW TESTAMENT BIBLE VERSES

9 Who shall be punished with everlasting destruction from the presence of the Lord, and from the glory of his power;

Jude 1:7 KJV / 778

7 Even as Sodom and Gomorrha, and the cities about them in like manner, giving themselves over to fornication, and going after strange flesh, are set forth for an example, suffering the vengeance of eternal fire.

Jude 1:12-13 KJV / 255

12 These are spots in your feasts of charity, when they feast with you, feeding themselves without fear: clouds they are without water, carried about of winds; trees whose fruit withereth, without fruit, twice dead, plucked up by the roots;

13 Raging waves of the sea, foaming out their own shame; wandering stars, to whom is reserved the blackness of darkness for ever.

PART 6
NEW TESTAMENT BIBLE VERSES

PART 6 NEW TESTAMENT BIBLE VERSES

The book of Revelation

Revelation 21:8 KJV / 1,741

8 But the fearful, and unbelieving, and the abominable, and murderers, and whoremongers, and sorcerers, and idolaters, and all liars, shall have their part in the lake which burneth with fire and brimstone: which is the second death.

Revelation 19:20 KJV / 688

20 And the beast was taken, and with him the false prophet that wrought miracles before him, with which he deceived them that had received the mark of the beast, and them that worshipped his image. These both were cast alive into a lake of fire burning with brimstone.

Revelation 2:10-11 KJV / 194

10 Fear none of those things which thou shalt suffer: behold, the devil shall cast some of you into prison, that ye may be tried; and ye shall have tribulation ten days: be thou faithful unto death, and I will give thee a crown of life.

PART 6 NEW TESTAMENT BIBLE VERSES

11 He that hath an ear, let him hear what the Spirit saith unto the churches; He that overcometh shall not be hurt of the second death.

Revelation 14:10-11 KJV / 360

10 The same shall drink of the wine of the wrath of God, which is poured out without mixture into the cup of his indignation; and he shall be tormented with fire and brimstone in the presence of the holy angels, and in the presence of the Lamb:

11 And the smoke of their torment ascendeth up for ever and ever: and they have no rest day nor night, who worship the beast and his image, and whosoever receiveth the mark of his name.

Revelation 3:8-16

8 I know thy works: behold, I have set before thee an open door, and no man can shut it: for thou hast a little strength, and hast kept my word, and hast not denied my name.

PART 6 NEW TESTAMENT BIBLE VERSES

9 Behold, I will make them of the synagogue of Satan, which say they are Jews, and are not, but do lie; behold, I will make them to come and worship before thy feet, and to know that I have loved thee.

10 Because thou hast kept the word of my patience, I also will keep thee from the hour of temptation, which shall come upon all the world, to try them that dwell upon the earth.

11 Behold, I come quickly: hold that fast which thou hast, that no man take thy crown.

12 Him that overcometh will I make a pillar in the temple of my God, and he shall go no more out: and I will write upon him the name of my God, and the name of the city of my God, which is new Jerusalem, which cometh down out of heaven from my God: and I will write upon him my new name.

13 He that hath an ear, let him hear what the Spirit saith unto the churches.

PART 6 NEW TESTAMENT BIBLE VERSES

14 And unto the angel of the church of the Laodiceans write; These things saith the Amen, the faithful and true witness, the beginning of the creation of God;

15 I know thy works, that thou art neither cold nor hot: I would thou wert cold or hot.

16 So then because thou art lukewarm, and neither cold nor hot, I will spue thee out of my mouth.

Revelation 20:1-15 KJV / 325

And I saw an angel come down from heaven, having the key of the bottomless pit and a great chain in his hand.

2 And he laid hold on the dragon, that old serpent, which is the Devil, and Satan, and bound him a thousand years,

3 And cast him into the bottomless pit, and shut him up, and set a seal upon him, that he should deceive the nations no more, till the thousand years should be fulfilled: and after that he must be loosed a little season.

PART 6 NEW TESTAMENT BIBLE VERSES

4 And I saw thrones, and they sat upon them, and judgment was given unto them: and I saw the souls of them that were beheaded for the witness of Jesus, and for the word of God, and which had not worshipped the beast, neither his image, neither had received his mark upon their foreheads, or in their hands; and they lived and reigned with Christ a thousand years.

5 But the rest of the dead lived not again until the thousand years were finished. This is the first resurrection.

6 Blessed and holy is he that hath part in the first resurrection: on such the second death hath no power, but they shall be priests of God and of Christ, and shall reign with him a thousand years.

7 And when the thousand years are expired, Satan shall be loosed out of his prison,

8 And shall go out to deceive the nations which are in the four quarters of the earth, Gog, and Magog, to gather them together to battle: the number of whom is as the sand of the sea.

PART 6 NEW TESTAMENT BIBLE VERSES

9 And they went up on the breadth of the earth, and compassed the camp of the saints about, and the beloved city: and fire came down from God out of heaven, and devoured them.

10 And the devil that deceived them was cast into the lake of fire and brimstone, where the beast and the false prophet are, and shall be tormented day and night for ever and ever.

11 And I saw a great white throne, and him that sat on it, from whose face the earth and the heaven fled away; and there was found no place for them.

12 And I saw the dead, small and great, stand before God; and the books were opened: and another book was opened, which is the book of life: and the dead were judged out of those things which were written in the books, according to their works.

13 And the sea gave up the dead which were in it; and death and hell delivered up the dead which were in them: and they were judged every man according to their works.

PART 6 NEW TESTAMENT BIBLE VERSES

14 And death and hell were cast into the lake of fire. This is the second death.

15 And whosoever was not found written in the book of life was cast into the lake of fire.

Revelation 1:1-20 KJV / 240

The Revelation of Jesus Christ, which God gave unto him, to shew unto his servants things which must shortly come to pass; and he sent and signified it by his angel unto his servant John:

2 Who bare record of the word of God, and of the testimony of Jesus Christ, and of all things that he saw.

3 Blessed is he that readeth, and they that hear the words of this prophecy, and keep those things which are written therein: for the time is at hand.

4 John to the seven churches which are in Asia: Grace be unto you, and peace, from him which is, and which was, and which is to come; and from the seven Spirits which are before his throne;

PART 6 NEW TESTAMENT BIBLE VERSES

5 And from Jesus Christ, who is the faithful witness, and the first begotten of the dead, and the prince of the kings of the earth. Unto him that loved us, and washed us from our sins in his own blood,

6 And hath made us kings and priests unto God and his Father; to him be glory and dominion for ever and ever. Amen.

7 Behold, he cometh with clouds; and every eye shall see him, and they also which pierced him: and all kindreds of the earth shall wail because of him. Even so, Amen.

8 I am Alpha and Omega, the beginning and the ending, saith the Lord, which is, and which was, and which is to come, the Almighty.

9 I John, who also am your brother, and companion in tribulation, and in the kingdom and patience of Jesus Christ, was in the isle that is called Patmos, for the word of God, and for the testimony of Jesus Christ.

10 I was in the Spirit on the Lord's day, and heard behind me a great voice, as of a trumpet,

PART 6 NEW TESTAMENT BIBLE VERSES

11 Saying, I am Alpha and Omega, the first and the last: and, What thou seest, write in a book, and send it unto the seven churches which are in Asia; unto Ephesus, and unto Smyrna, and unto Pergamos, and unto Thyatira, and unto Sardis, and unto Philadelphia, and unto Laodicea.

12 And I turned to see the voice that spake with me. And being turned, I saw seven golden candlesticks;

13 And in the midst of the seven candlesticks one like unto the Son of man, clothed with a garment down to the foot, and girt about the paps with a golden girdle.

14 His head and his hairs were white like wool, as white as snow; and his eyes were as a flame of fire;

15 And his feet like unto fine brass, as if they burned in a furnace; and his voice as the sound of many waters.

16 And he had in his right hand seven stars: and out of his mouth went a sharp twoedged sword: and his countenance was as the sun shineth in his strength.

PART 6 NEW TESTAMENT BIBLE VERSES

17 And when I saw him, I fell at his feet as dead. And he laid his right hand upon me, saying unto me, Fear not; I am the first and the last:

18 I am he that liveth, and was dead; and, behold, I am alive for evermore, Amen; and have the keys of hell and of death.

19 Write the things which thou hast seen, and the things which are, and the things which shall be hereafter;

20 The mystery of the seven stars which thou sawest in my right hand, and the seven golden candlesticks. The seven stars are the angels of the seven churches: and the seven candlesticks which thou sawest are the seven churches.

PART 7
BIBLE LIFE
LESSON ON HELL

PART 7 BIBLE LIFE LESSON
THE RICH MAN & LAZARUS

Luke 16:19-31 KJV / 613

19 There was a certain rich man, which was clothed in purple and fine linen, and fared sumptuously every day:

20 And there was a certain beggar named Lazarus, which was laid at his gate, full of sores,

21 And desiring to be fed with the crumbs which fell from the rich man's table: moreover the dogs came and licked his sores.

22 And it came to pass, that the beggar died, and was carried by the angels into Abraham's bosom: the rich man also died, and was buried;

23 And in hell he lift up his eyes, being in torments, and seeth Abraham afar off, and Lazarus in his bosom.

24 And he cried and said, Father Abraham, have mercy on me, and send Lazarus, that he may dip the tip of his finger in water, and cool my tongue; for I am tormented in this flame.

PART 7 BIBLE LIFE LESSON
THE RICH MAN & LAZARUS

25 But Abraham said, Son, remember that thou in thy lifetime receivedst thy good things, and likewise Lazarus evil things: but now he is comforted, and thou art tormented.

26 And beside all this, between us and you there is a great gulf fixed: so that they which would pass from hence to you cannot; neither can they pass to us, that would come from thence.

27 Then he said, I pray thee therefore, father, that thou wouldest send him to my father's house:

28 For I have five brethren; that he may testify unto them, lest they also come into this place of torment.

29 Abraham saith unto him, They have Moses and the prophets; let them hear them.

30 And he said, Nay, father Abraham: but if one went unto them from the dead, they will repent.
31 And he said unto him, If they hear not Moses and the prophets, neither will they be persuaded, though one rose from the dead.

PART 7 BIBLE LIFE LESSON
THE RICH MAN & LAZARUS

Some believe this story is a parable, others believe that since Jesus rarely used names in parables that it is an actual account. Either way there are some amazing take aways from this story.

Luke 16:24

* The rich man had an attitude of being served and not serving. He requested Abraham to assist in getting Lazaurus to serve him water.

Luke 16:26

* There is a great gulf fixed that can not be crossed once you die.

Luke 16:28

* These event take place in real time, because the rich man was aware that his brothers were still alive and living at his father's house.

Hebrews 9:27 And as it is appointed unto men once to die, but after this the judgment:

PART 7 BIBLE LIFE LESSON
THE RICH MAN & LAZARUS

* the judgement. It appears a judgement is made not long after you die.

Luke 16:26-28

Based on verse 26-28 ...You should have a sense of urgency about spreading the gospel of Jesus Christ to loved ones now. You can't do it, or send someone to do it, after you are dead.

Luke 16:31

* There is no "Forced Entry" with God. There is nothing more powerful than the word of God when it comes to salvation. However there are some loved ones you will not be able to reach. They have free will the same as you. "If they hear not Moses and the prophets, neither will they be persuaded, though one rose from the dead."

In Conclusion

This story has a similar message as the timeless Christmas classic Scrooge. Where Scrooge was led by spirits to see the current path he was on, led to future torment. Like Scrooge, when the rich man experienced the torment, he wanted to help others. Only in this reality there was no second chance.

PART 7 BIBLE LIFE LESSON
THE RICH MAN & LAZARUS

He and likely his five brothers would end up in eternal torment.

A long time ago a person told me, if life was getting me down, to purchase the Sunday newspaper and read the Obituary section. There, no matter what I was going through, I would see a page full of people of which the majority would gladly trade places with me.

Matthew 7:14 Because strait is the gate, and narrow is the way, which leadeth unto life, and few there be that find it.

The message being, today is the day of salvation, tomorrow may be too late.

"Whereas ye know not what shall be on the morrow. For what is your life? It is even a vapour, that appeareth for a little time, and then vanisheth away." James 4:14

PART 8 Top 10 Bible Verses on Hell

PART 8 TOP 10 BIBLE VERSES ON HELL

Here is the top 10 list of bible verses on Hell as voted on by Christians around the world

10.   2 Thessalonians 1:9 KJV / 945

9 Who shall be punished with everlasting destruction from the presence of the Lord, and from the glory of his power;

9.   Revelation 14:11 KJV / 1,018

11 And the smoke of their torment ascendeth up for ever and ever: and they have no rest day nor night, who worship the beast and his image, and whosoever receiveth the mark of his name.

8.   Matthew 5:22 KJV / 1,061

22 But I say unto you, That whosoever is angry with his brother without a cause shall be in danger of the judgment: and whosoever shall say to his brother, Raca, shall be in danger of the council: but whosoever shall say, Thou fool, shall be in danger of hell fire.

PART 8 TOP 10 BIBLE VERSES ON HELL

7.   Revelation 20:15 KJV / 1,096

15 And whosoever was not found written in the book of life was cast into the lake of fire.

6.   Matthew 25:41 KJV / 1,139

41 Then shall he say also unto them on the left hand, Depart from me, ye cursed, into everlasting fire, prepared for the devil and his angels:

5.   Romans 6:23 KJV / 1,212

23 For the wages of sin is death; but the gift of God is eternal life through Jesus Christ our Lord.

4.   Revelation 20:10 KJV / 1,308

10 And the devil that deceived them was cast into the lake of fire and brimstone, where the beast and the false prophet are, and shall be tormented day and night for ever and ever.

PART 8 TOP 10 BIBLE VERSES ON HELL

3. Matthew 25:46 KJV / 1,444

46 And these shall go away into everlasting punishment: but the righteous into life eternal.

2. Matthew 10:28 KJV / 1,534

28 And fear not them which kill the body, but are not able to kill the soul: but rather fear him which is able to destroy both soul and body in hell.

1. Revelation 21:8 KJV / 1,741

8 But the fearful, and unbelieving, and the abominable, and murderers, and whoremongers, and sorcerers, and idolaters, **and** all liars, shall have their part in the lake which burneth with fire and brimstone: which is the second death.

PART 8 TOP 10 BIBLE VERSES ON HELL

A few questions about the top 10 bible verses about Hell.

Do you agree on this list?

Do you have a scripture that you believe should be in the top 10? If so, why?

How do these top 10 scriptures make you feel about Hell?

a. I am afraid
b. not worried at all
c. somewhat worried
d. my election is sure

How do you think God wants you to feel about Hell?

If you are uncomfortable about Hell then close your eyes for a moment and imagine that you are the rich man from Luke chapter 16, only today, you have a 2nd chance... now, what changes in your life, if any, will you do avoid his fate?

PART 8 TOP 10 BIBLE VERSES ON HELL

Because we all have an appointment that none of us are going to miss.

Hebrews 9:27

And as it is appointed unto men once to die, but after this the judgment:

PART 9
Bible Quiz on Hell

PART 9 BIBLE QUIZ ON HELL

Welcome to the quiz on bible verses about Hell. You are going to have ten quick & easy review questions. There will bbe at least one question from each section of the entire book.

OK Let's begin!

1. Which bible verse says:
Isaiah 5:14 KJV / 265
14 Therefore hell hath enlarged herself, and opened her mouth without measure: and their glory, and their multitude, and their pomp, and he that rejoiceth, shall descend into it.

- a. Genesis   5:14
- b. Daniel   5:14
- c. Revelation   5:14
- d. Isaiah   5:14

2. Which bible verse says:
Psalm 9:17 KJV / 456
17 The wicked shall be turned into hell, and all the nations that forget God.

PART 9 BIBLE QUIZ ON HELL

a. Psalm 9:17
b. Proverbs 9:17
c. Revelation 9:17
d. Matthew 9:17

3. What bible verse says:
Matthew 10:28 KJV / 1,534

28 And fear not them which kill the body, but are not able to kill the soul: but rather fear him which is able to destroy both soul and body in hell.

a. Revelation 10:28
b. Matthew 10:28
c. Luke 10:28
d. Jude 10:28

4. What bible verse says:
Acts 2:31 KJV / 396

31 He seeing this before spake of the resurrection of Christ, that his soul was not left in hell, neither his flesh did see corruption.

PART 9 BIBLE QUIZ ON HELL

    a. Revelation   2:10
    b. Matthew   7:14
    c. Acts   2:31
    d. Acts   2:36

5. What bible verse says:

Revelation 2:10-11 KJV / 194
10 Fear none of those things which thou shalt suffer: behold, the devil shall cast some of you into prison, that ye may be tried; and ye shall have tribulation ten days: be thou faithful unto death, and I will give thee a crown of life.

11 He that hath an ear, let him hear what the Spirit saith unto the churches; He that overcometh shall not be hurt of the second death.

    a. Matthew   2:10-11
    b. 1 John   2:10-11
    c. Daniel   2:10-11
    d. Revelation   2:10-11

PART 9 BIBLE QUIZ ON HELL

6. Which Bible Verse was voted the number 2 bible verse on hell ?

a. Matthew 10:28
b. Genesis 10:28
c. 1 Corinthians 10:28
d. Revelation 10:28

28 And fear not them which kill the body, but are not able to kill the soul: but rather fear him which is able to destroy both soul and body in hell.

7. Which Bible Verse was voted the number 1 bible verse on hell?

a. Isaiah 21:8
b. Matthew 21:8
c. Revelation 21:8
d. Daniel 21:8

PART 9 BIBLE QUIZ ON HELL

8. Fill in the blank:

Revelation 3:15-16
15 I know thy works, that thou art neither cold nor hot: I would thou wert cold or hot.
16 So then _____thou art _____, and neither cold nor hot, I will spue thee _____ of my mouth.

a. if, fearful, out
b. when, warm, into
c. because, lukewarm, out
d. because, sinful, out

9. Question from the Life Lesson:
Why couldn't Abraham help the Rich Man get water?

a. Because the rich man was given good things and did not share.
b. Because there is a uncrossable barrier in the torment section of hell.
c. Because the rich man was never baptised into Jesus Christ.
d. Because the rich man had not completed his time in purgatory.

d.

PART 9 BIBLE QUIZ ON HELL

10. Question from the Life Lesson
Why wouldn't Abraham help the rich man's five brothers?

a. The five brothers were sinful like the rich man.
b. Because the five brothers were rich as well.
c. Because there is a great gulf fixed & they rejected the word of God.
d. The five brothers never worshipped God.

If you got all of the questions right, congratulations! If not, then continue to study you will get better!

2 Timothy 2:15
Study to shew thyself approved unto God, a workman that needeth not to be ashamed, rightly dividing the word of truth.

Romans 10:17
So then faith cometh by hearing, and hearing by the word of God.

BIBLE QUIZ ANSWERS

1. Which bible verse says:

Isaiah 5:14 KJV / 265
14 Therefore hell hath enlarged herself, and opened her mouth without measure: and their glory, and their multitude, and their pomp, and he that rejoiceth, shall descend into it.

The correct answer to this question is...
d. Isaiah 5:14

2. Which bible verse says:

Psalm 9:17 KJV / 456
17 The wicked shall be turned into hell, and all the nations that forget God.

The correct answer to this question is...
a. Psalm   9:17

3. What bible verse says:

Matthew 10:28 KJV / 1,534
28 And fear not them which kill the body, but are not able to kill the soul: but rather fear him which is able to destroy both soul and body in hell.

The correct answer to this question is...
b. Matthew   10:28

BIBLE QUIZ ANSWERS

4. What bible verse says:

Acts 2:31 KJV / 396
31 He seeing this before spake of the resurrection of Christ, that his soul was not left in hell, neither his flesh did see corruption.

The correct answer to this question is...
c. Acts 2:31

5. What bible verse says:

Revelation 2:10-11 KJV / 194

10 Fear none of those things which thou shalt suffer: behold, the devil shall cast some of you into prison, that ye may be tried; and ye shall have tribulation ten days: be thou faithful unto death, and I will give thee a crown of life.
11 He that hath an ear, let him hear what the Spirit saith unto the churches; He that overcometh shall not be hurt of the second death.

The correct answer to this question is...
d. Revelation 2:10-11

6. Which Bible Verse was voted the number 2 bible verse on hell ?

The correct answer to this question is...
a. Matthew 10:28

28 And fear not them which kill the body, but are not able to kill the soul: but rather fear him which is able to destroy both soul and body in hell.

BIBLE QUIZ ANSWERS

7. Which Bible Verse was voted the number 1 bible verse on hell?

1.   Revelation 21:8 KJV / 1,741

8 But the fearful, and unbelieving, and the abominable, and murderers, and whoremongers, and sorcerers, and idolaters, and all liars, shall have their part in the lake which burneth with fire and brimstone: which is the second death.

The correct answer to this question is...
c. Revelation 21:8

8. Fill in the blank:

Revelation 3:15-16
15 I know thy works, that thou art neither cold nor hot: I would thou wert cold or hot.
16 So then _____thou art _____, and neither cold nor hot, I will spue thee _____ of my mouth.

The correct answer to this question is...
c. because, lukewarm, out

Revelation 3:15-16
15 I know thy works, that thou art neither cold nor hot: I would thou wert cold or hot.
16 So then **because** thou art **lukewarm**, and neither cold nor hot, I will spue thee **out** of my mouth.

BIBLE QUIZ ANSWERS

9. Question from the Life Lesson:

Why couldn't Abraham help the Rich Man get water?

The correct answer to this question is...
b. Because there is a uncrossable barrier in the torment section of hell.

Luke 16:26 And beside all this, between us and you there is a great gulf fixed: so that they which would pass from hence to you cannot; neither can they pass to us, that would come from thence.

10. Question from the Life Lesson
Why wouldn't Abraham help the rich man's five brothers?

The correct answer to this question is...
c. Because there is a great gulf fixed & they rejected the word of God.

Luke 16:26 And beside all this, between us and you there is a great gulf fixed: so that they which would pass from hence to you cannot; neither can they pass to us, that would come from thence.

Luke 16:31 And he said unto him, If they hear not Moses and the prophets, neither will they be persuaded, though one rose from the dead.

PART 10
CONCLUSION

PART 10 CONCLUSION

I want to thank you for completing this book on the Bible Verses about **Hell.**

Now you have the knowledge of...

* The best Old Testament Bible Verses on **this amazing topic**!

* The best New Testament Bible Verses on this amazing topic!

* The top 10 Scriptures as voted on worldwide!

* Knowledge of an Amazing Bible story or scriptures that do a great job to best illustrate & help you to understand about **Hell**!

* Increased knowledge that you can now share with family, friends, and the world!

You have taken a step forward to being ready to give an answer to every man that asketh you a reason for the hope that is in you.... **1 Peter 3:15**

You have taken the time to grow spiritually so you can share the good news of Jesus the Christ and the Word of God.

Romans 10:17

So then faith cometh by hearing, and hearing by the word of God.

You have increased your faith!

PART 10 CONCLUSION

But don't let this be the end! Be like those in Berea...

Acts 17:10-11

10 And the brethren immediately sent away Paul and Silas by night unto Berea: who coming thither went into the synagogue of the Jews.

11 These were more noble than those in Thessalonica, in that they received the word with all readiness of mind, and searched the scriptures daily, whether those things were so.

This is only one of what will be a 40 book library of books covering the many fasinating topics in the Bible.

Thanks again...and may God continue to guide, guard and protect you and yours.

Now let me leave you with this encouraging scripture about the power of recieving the word of God both day and night.

Psalm 1:1-3

1 Blessed is the man that walketh not in the counsel of the ungodly, nor standeth in the way of sinners, nor sitteth in the seat of the scornful.

2 But his delight is in the law of the Lord; and in his law doth he meditate day and night.

3 And he shall be like a tree planted by the rivers of water, that bringeth forth his fruit in his season; his leaf also shall not wither; and whatsoever he doeth shall prosper.

We want to thank you for the purchase of this book and more importantly, thank you for reading it to the end. We hope your reading experience was pleasurable and that you would inform your family and friends on Facebook, Twitter or other social media.

We would like to continue to provide you with high-quality books, and that end, would you mind leaving us a review on Amazon.com?

Just use the link below, scroll down about 3/4 of the page and you will see images similar to the one below.

We are extremely grateful for your assistance.
Warm Regards, MahoneyProducts Publishing

Book Link:
https://www.amazon.com/dp/B0BB5YL2L2
Customer reviews
4.6 out of 5 stars

4.6 out of 5
6 global ratings

5 star   %_
star   %-
star 0% (0%)   %
star 0% (0%)   %
star 0% (0%)

You might also enjoy:

Christian Book Series Self Help Bible Study Guide on Heaven

KJV Bible Based Verses & Lessons for Men, Women, Couples, Teens, Kids, & Beginners

by Brian Mahoney

Christian Marriage Counseling Book of Bible Verses:

Marriage Scriptures to help Women, Men, Kids, Moms & Couples with Intimacy, Sex & Communication

Paperback – November 5, 2021

by Brian Mahoney (Author)

4.5 out of 5 stars with 25 ratings

Marriage Book Amazon Link:

https://www.amazon.com/dp/B09L3NNZRR

Please leave a review

http://amazon.com/review/create-review/asin=B0B93G59J8

and then join Our VIP Mailing List Then Get Notified when we release our new books on FREE promotions.

FREE Amazon ebooks and free Audible ACX audio books!

Just click or Type in the Link Below

https://urlzs.com/HfbGF

www.ingramcontent.com/pod-product-compliance
Lightning Source LLC
Chambersburg PA
CBHW072040110526
44592CB00012B/1501